KATHY and DAVID BLACKW

CW00539373

SOLO TIME FOR CELLO

BOOK 1

Contents

Grateful thanks are due to Alison Ingram for all her help with this collection.

Audio: there are full performances and piano-only backings for each piece in this collection at www.oup.com/solocello1. Audio credits: Laura Anstee (cello), David Blackwell (piano), Ken Blair (producer/engineer for BMP The Sound Recording Company Ltd.). Recorded at the Holywell Music Room, Oxford.

Repeats, Da Capos, and Dal Segnos are observed for each piece in the recordings, except for No. 11.

OXFORD
UNIVERSITY PRESS

Great Clarendon Street, Oxford OX2 6DP, England.

ISBN 978-0-19-355066-7
Music and text origination by Julia Bovee
Printed in Great Britain

1. Gavotte 1

from Orchestral Suite No. 3, BWV 1068

Johann Sebastian Bach (1685–1750)

arr. KB & DB

Bach's four orchestral suites showcase movements based on dances, such as this lively Gavotte, a dance in duple time which usually begins, as this one does, on the half bar. Along with other dance forms, it was widely used by Baroque composers in their instrumental works. Play at a brisk pace with a strong sense of two beats in a bar/ measure and capture the dance-like feeling by playing in a lightly detached manner. Dynamics are suggestions only.

2. Contredanse

No. 6 from *12 Contredanses*, WoO 14

Ludwig van Beethoven (1770–1827)
arr. KB & DB

Probably the most well-known of all classical composers, Beethoven wrote prolifically in a range of musical genres, from large-scale symphonies to concertos, sonatas, and songs. The practice of composing suites of *Contredanses* (country dances), where stylized forms of folk tunes, usually in binary form, were arranged for orchestra,

was popular with composers in the eighteenth century, including Haydn, Mozart, and Beethoven. This piece, arranged from the orchestral original, is typical of the form, with two contrasted dances, each in binary form with repeated sections.

3. Two Dances
from *Terpsichore*

Pierre-Francisque Caroubel (1549–1611)
arr. KB & DB

1. L'Espagnollette

2. Courrant de Mons

Michael Praetorius (1571–1621)
arr. KB & DB

Terpsichore, published in 1612, is a collection of 312 French courtly dance tunes compiled and arranged by the German composer Michael Praetorius. The collection is named after the Greek muse of dance. Pieces in the collection that are marked F. C. are believed to be entirely written by Pierre-Francisque Caroubel, a violinist in the French court, and those marked M. P. C. to have been arranged by Praetorius himself. The L'Espagnollette is a lively Spanish-style dance from a category of the collection that Praetorius described as 'dances with strange names' and the Courrant is a fast lively dance.

4.   O Ruddier than the Cherry

from *Acis and Galatea* HWV 49

George Frederick Handel (1685–1759)

arr. KB & DB

Although he was born in Germany, Handel spent most of his life living and working in England where he composed operas and many large-scale choral works based on biblical themes, such as the oratorio *Messiah*. 'O Ruddier than the Cherry' is an arrangement of a dramatic bass aria originally sung by the character Polyphemus, from the opera *Acis and Galatea*, first performed in 1718. The opera tells the love story of two characters from Greek mythology—Acis, a mortal shepherd, and Galatea, a semi-divine nymph. The pastoral and gentle story later takes a dramatic turn when the giant Polyphemus, who loves Galatea, murders Acis in a jealous rage.

5. Columbine

from *Children's Carnival*, Op. 25 No. 2

Amy Beach (1867–1944)
arr. KB & DB

The American composer and pianist Amy Beach is considered the first successful female American composer of large-scale classical music, and her 'Gaelic' symphony, first published and performed in 1896, was the first symphony to have been written by a female American composer. She wrote many pieces for piano and *Columbine* is from a collection of short pieces for young players. The title refers to a female archetypal character in the Commedia dell' Arte, a type of theatrical entertainment popular in Europe from the 16th to the 18th century, which originated in Italy. Commedia dell' Arte featured stock characters such as the wise old man and Pierrot the sad clown who pines for the love of Columbine, who often breaks his heart.

6. Little Hungarian Rhapsody

Carl Bohm (1844–1920)
adapted and arr. KB & DB

Carl Bohm was a German composer famous for his many songs and instrumental works written in a light salon-style vein. The exotic nature of Hungarian-style music, with its contrasts of mood and speed, was very popular with composers in the nineteenth century, though in fact Bohm begins this piece, originally written for violin and piano, with a mazurka, which is a traditional Polish dance! Enjoy the contrasts of mood, key, and tempo. In the mazurka, articulate the ♪♪ rhythms cleanly. By way of contrast, play bars 27–9 in free time with a feeling of improvisation. The final 'Allegro vivace' section contrasts the changes from major to minor. Play the final chords strongly for an exciting finish.

7. Die Lotosblume

from *Myrthen*, Op. 25 No. 7

Robert Schumann (1810–56)
arr. KB & DB

Robert Schumann is widely considered to be one of the foremost composers of the Romantic era, writing both orchestral and piano music, and numerous *Lieder*, songs for voice and piano. *Die Lotosblume*, the lotus flower, is an arrangement of a song from a collection that Schumann dedicated and presented to his wife Clara, also a composer and virtuoso pianist, on the occasion of their wedding in 1840. *Myrthen*—myrtles—are evergreen plants traditionally used as a symbol for marriage.

8. Joshua fit the battle of Jericho

Spiritual
arr. KB & DB

The words of this spiritual recall the biblical story in which Joshua and the Israelites fought ('fit') and won a famous victory at Jericho over the Canaanites. According to the story, the walls of the city fell after Joshua's army marched around them blowing trumpets. It has been seen as a metaphor for escape from slavery. This energetic arrangement needs to be played with a strong sense of jazz/blues style—bars 31–4 are like a written-out improvisation. The ♪s should be played evenly ('straight') and not swung. Enjoy the glissando in bar 43 as the walls come tumbling down!

9. Intermezzo

from *Cavalleria rusticana*

Pietro Mascagni (1863–1945)
arr. KB & DB

Pietro Mascagni was an Italian composer and conductor who wrote fifteen operas, as well as orchestral and chamber music. This Intermezzo, an interlude between theatrical scenes, is from one of his most well-known compositions, the one-act opera *Cavalleria rusticana* (Rustic chivalry), first performed in 1890. It is a story of love, betrayal, and revenge set in Sicily in the nineteenth century. This lyrical and heart-rending piece is perhaps the most famous and widely known part of the opera.

10. Adoration

Florence B. Price (1887–1953)
arr. KB & DB

The composer Florence B. Price is famous for being the first African-American composer to have a major symphonic work performed by a professional orchestra. While a student at the New England Conservatory of Music in Boston, she is said to have passed herself as Mexican in order to avoid the racial discrimination of the times. She was both a talented pianist and organist, and this lyrical piece is an arrangement of a piece originally written for organ.

11. Vivace

third movement of Sonata Op. 1 No. 2

Amélie-Julie Candeille (1767–1834)
adapted and arr. KB & DB

The French child prodigy Amélie-Julie Candeille was not only a composer of keyboard music and music for the stage but also a singer, pianist, actor, and playwright. Her keyboard works, often written for her own personal performance, are virtuosic in style and display a straightforward use of harmony. This piece is an arrangement and adaptation of a sonata movement originally written for harpsichord.

12. Libera me

from *Requiem*, Op. 48

Gabriel Fauré (1845–1924)
arr. KB & DB

Gabriel Fauré was a French composer who trained as a church musician. These two pieces, from his *Requiem* for choir and orchestra composed around 1888, are arrangements of the final two movements. *Libera me*, sung first by a baritone solo, asks God to have mercy upon the deceased person, while *In paradisum* is a prayer of consolation sung by the sopranos with the text 'may the angels lead you into paradise'. Contrast the darker and more dramatic mood of *Libera me* with the solace and gentle expressiveness of *In paradisum*. To help shape the phrases, imagine where a singer might breathe.

13. In paradisum

from *Requiem*, Op. 48

Gabriel Fauré (1845–1924)

arr. KB & DB

14. Pièce Romantique

Op. 9 No. 1

Cécile Chaminade (1857–1944)
arr. KB & DB

The French pianist and composer Cécile Chaminade began her musical studies with her mother, as her father disapproved of her having a musical education; she later attended the Paris conservatoire. She is mostly well known as a composer of short pieces for piano, although she also composed more substantial pieces, such as her piano trio and concertino for flute and orchestra. She had considerable success as both a composer and performer at the start of the twentieth century, giving recitals in the USA and England. This tuneful piece is from a set of two pieces for piano.

15. Le Pique-nique

from *Sports et divertissements*

Erik Satie (1866–1925)
arr. KB & DB

[1] They all brought very cold veal.   [2] You have a beautiful white dress.   [3] Here! An aeroplane.   [4] Oh no: it's a thunderstorm.

Sports et divertissements depicts a variety of sports and pastimes (tennis, golf, sea bathing, etc.) in 21 short, humorous piano pieces, each with a prose poem by Satie. Written in 1914, it was finally published in 1923 in an illustrated edition that reproduced Satie's beautifully handwritten scores in facsimile. Satie dispensed with barlines and key signatures throughout, but we've added both here, partly for ease of reading and not least as the piece fits nicely into a jaunty ragtime rhythm. In this piece a pleasant day out is abruptly cut short by the weather.

16. Idylle Haïtienne

from *La flamenca*

Lucien Lambert (1858–1945)
arr. KB & DB

Lucien Lambert was a French pianist and composer of African-American descent. His father, also a pianist and composer, grew up in New Orleans but moved to France, where Lucien was born. Lucien studied at the Paris conservatoire and is believed to be one of the first classical pianists of African heritage to have made recordings. This beautifully expressive piece, from Act II of his opera *La flamenca*, conveys the languorous natural beauty of Haiti. It is one of a set of Creole dances (Danses Créoles) that depict the styles of different Caribbean and Latin American countries.

17. Russian Dance

from *Danse caractéristique*, Op. 2 No. 6

Vladimir Ivanovich Rebikov (1866–1920)

arr. KB & DB

This lively Russian dance is from a set of 'Characteristic Dances' for piano by the Russian composer Vladimir Ivanovich Rebikov. Capture the strong rhythms and folk style with strong accents and energetic bowing. By way of contrast, aim for a legato and gentle sound in the 'Meno mosso' section.

KATHY and DAVID BLACKWELL

SOLO TIME FOR CELLO

BOOK 1

Piano accompaniment book

Contents

Grateful thanks are due to Alison Ingram for all her help with this collection.

OXFORD
UNIVERSITY PRESS

Great Clarendon Street, Oxford OX2 6DP, England.
This collection and each individual work within it © Oxford University Press 2022.
Unauthorized arrangement or photocopying of this copyright material is ILLEGAL.

Kathy and David Blackwell have asserted their right under the Copyright, Designs and Patents Act,
1988, to be identified as the Authors of this Work.

ISBN 978-0-19-355066-7
Music and text origination by Julia Bovee
Printed in Great Britain

1. Gavotte 1

from Orchestral Suite No. 3, BWV 1068

Johann Sebastian Bach (1685–1750)
arr. KB & DB

2. Contredanse

No. 6 from *12 Contredanses*, WoO 14

Ludwig van Beethoven (1770–1827)

arr. KB & DB

Trio

D.C. al Fine

5

3. Two Dances

from *Terpsichore*

Pierre-Francisque Caroubel (1549–1611)
arr. KB & DB

1. L'Espagnollette

2. Courrant de Mons

Michael Praetorius (1571–1621)
arr. KB & DB

4. O Ruddier than the Cherry

from Acis and Galatea HWV 49

George Frederick Handel (1685–1759)
arr. KB & DB

5. Columbine

from *Children's Carnival,* Op. 25 No. 2

Amy Beach (1867–1944)
arr. KB & DB

6. Little Hungarian Rhapsody

Carl Bohm (1844–1920)
adapted and arr. KB & DB

7. Die Lotosblume

from *Myrthen*, Op. 25 No. 7

Robert Schumann (1810–56)
arr. KB & DB

8. Joshua fit the battle of Jericho

Spiritual
arr. KB & DB

9. Intermezzo

from *Cavalleria rusticana*

Pietro Mascagni (1863–1945)
arr. KB & DB

10. Adoration

Florence B. Price (1887–1953)
arr. KB & DB

11. Vivace

third movement of Sonata Op. 1 No. 2

Amélie-Julie Candeille (1767–1834)
adapted and arr. KB & DB

12. Libera me

from *Requiem,* Op. 48

Gabriel Fauré (1845–1924)
arr. KB & DB

13. In paradisum

from *Requiem*, Op. 48

Gabriel Fauré (1845–1924)

arr. KB & DB

Andante moderato ♩ = 60

14. Pièce Romantique

Op. 9 No. 1

Cécile Chaminade (1857–1944)
arr. KB & DB

15. Le Pique-nique

from *Sports et divertissements*

Erik Satie (1866–1925)

arr. KB & DB

[1] They all brought very cold veal.   [2] You have a beautiful white dress.   [3] Here! An aeroplane.   [4] Oh no: it's a thunderstorm.

16. Idylle Haïtienne

from *La flamenca*

Lucien Lambert (1858–1945)
arr. KB & DB

17. Russian Dance

from *Danse caractéristique*, Op. 2 No. 6

Vladimir Ivanovich Rebikov (1866–1920)

arr. KB & DB

accelerando

sub. **p** cresc.

sub. **p** cresc.

40